INSIDE THE NFL

ATLANTA FALCONS

by Luke Hanlon

Abdo & Daughters
MIDDLE GRADE NONFICTION

An imprint of Abdo Publishing
abdobooks.com

ABDOBOOKS.COM

Published by Abdo Publishing, a division of ABDO, PO Box 398166, Minneapolis, Minnesota 55439.

Printed in China.
052025
092025

THIS BOOK CONTAINS RECYCLED MATERIALS

Cover Photos: Justin Casterline/Getty Images Sport/Getty Images (Bijan Robinson); Rob Carr/Getty Images Sport/Getty Images (Julio Jones)
Interior Photos: Rich von Biberstein/Icon Sportswire/Getty Images, 4–5; Wesley Hitt/Getty Images Sport/Getty Images, 6, 63; Stacy Revere/Getty Images Sport/Getty Images, 6–7; Ella Hall/Getty Images Sport/Getty Images, 7; Kevin C. Cox/Getty Images Sport/Getty Images, 8, 9, 50, 59; Abdo Publishing, 10–11; Charles E. Rotkin/Corbis Historical/VCG/Getty Images, 12–13; AP Images, 14, 15, 23, 27, 60 (bottom left); Vic Stein/Getty Images Sport/Getty Images, 16; Focus on Sport/Getty Images Sport/Getty Images, 17, 20, 21, 24–25, 27 (top), 31, 60 (top left); Focus on Sport/Getty Images, 18; George Gojkovich/Getty Images Sport/Getty Images, 19; Clifton Boutelle/Getty Images Sport/Getty Images, 22; Greg Trott/AP Images, 26; Paul Jasienski/AP Images, 28 (top); David Durochik/AP Images, 28 (bottom); Paul Spinelli/NFL Photos/AP Images, 29 (top); Allen Dean Steele/Getty Images Sport/Getty Images, 29 (bottom); Otto Greule Jr./Getty Images Sport/Getty Images, 30; Allen Kee/AP Images, 32–33; Tom Gannam/AP Images, 34; Alan Mothner/AP Images, 35; Rhona Wise/AFP/Getty Images, 36; Elsa Hasch/Allsport/Hulton Archive/Getty Images, 37; Andy Lyons/Allsport/Getty Images Sport/Getty Images, 38, 39; David Stluka/AP Images, 40; Al Bello/Getty Images Sport/Getty Images, 41, 60 (bottom right); Steve Schaefer/AFP/Getty Images, 42, 60 (top right); Streeter Lecka/Getty Images Sport/Getty Images, 43, 51; Scott Cunningham/Getty Images Sport/Getty Images, 44; Todd Kirkland/Icon SMI/Corbis/Icon Sportswire/Getty Images, 45; Icon Sportswire/Getty Images, 46–47, 61 (top left); Brian Garfinkel/AP Images, 48; Curtis Compton/Atlanta Journal-Constitution/AP Images, 49, 61 (bottom); Ryan Kang/AP Images, 52; G. Newman Lowrance/AP Images, 53, 61 (top right); Elise Amendola/AP Images, 54; Elsa/Getty Images Sport/Getty Images, 55; Patrick Smith/Getty Images Sport/Getty Images, 56; Grant Halverson/Getty Images Sport/Getty Images, 57; Shutterstock Images, 58

Editor: Rebecca Higgins
Series Designer: Laura Graphenteen
Production Designer: Katharine Hale

Library of Congress Control Number: 2024948480

Publisher's Cataloging-in-Publication Data

Names: Hanlon, Luke, author.
Title: Atlanta Falcons / by Luke Hanlon
Description: Minneapolis, Minnesota: Abdo Publishing, 2026 | Series: Inside the NFL | Includes online resources and index.
Identifiers: ISBN 9781098296636 (lib. bdg.) | ISBN 9798384919155 (ebook)
Subjects: LCSH: Atlanta Falcons (Football team)--Juvenile literature. | National Football League--Juvenile literature. | Football teams--Juvenile literature. | American football--Juvenile literature.
Classification: DDC 796.333--dc23

CONTENTS

Falcons running back Bijan Robinson recorded more than 100 total yards in six games as a rookie.

CHAPTER 1

CAN'T STOP BIJAN

ATLANTA FALCONS RUNNING BACK BIJAN ROBINSON RECEIVED A PITCH 6 yards behind the line of scrimmage. In no time, Green Bay Packers defensive end Kingsley Enagbare burst through the line and had a clean shot on Robinson in the backfield. But the Falcons rookie was out to prove himself during this Week 2 matchup in the 2023 season.

Robinson planted his right foot into the turf and juked hard to his left. Enagbare slipped and fell to his knees. Green Bay safety Darnell Savage sprinted up the field and dived toward Robinson. The agile back easily evaded the tackle by cutting quickly to his left.

Robinson sped down the field. When another Packers defender blocked his path, Robinson shifted to his left and ran free. By the time two Packers tackled Robinson, he had gained 19 yards and a first down.

Robinson scored eight touchdowns in 2023.

GENERATIONAL TALENT

Robinson first made a name for himself in college with the Texas Longhorns. In his final season, he led his conference with 1,580 rushing yards and 20 total touchdowns to earn All-American honors. Many analysts considered Robinson to be a top prospect for the 2023 National Football League (NFL) Draft that spring. In fact, some said Robinson was the most talented running back prospect in years. He combined elusiveness with an elite ability to run routes and catch the ball out of the backfield.

The Falcons were coming off a second consecutive 7–10 season. They had plenty of needs, and there was an opportunity to fill one of them with the eighth pick in the 2023 NFL Draft. But a running back didn't seem to be one of those needs. The Falcons already had Tyler Allgeier, who was coming off a rookie season in which he ran for more than 1,000 yards. However, when Robinson was still

Robinson impressed scouts at the 2023 NFL Combine.

Robinson, *left*, celebrates after scoring his first career touchdown.

available during Atlanta's pick, the team couldn't resist drafting the talented back.

WORTH THE PRICE

Robinson showed off his abilities right away in his NFL debut. Splitting carries with Allgeier, the rookie gained 83 total yards and scored a touchdown. Fans were eager to see what he would do in Week 2 when the Packers came to town. Robinson was ready.

Green Bay took an early 10–3 lead in the game. Late in the second quarter, the Falcons started a drive on their own 25-yard line. Over four carries, Robinson picked up 30 yards. When the Falcons faced fourth-and-one on Green Bay's 26, Atlanta head coach Arthur Smith called another play for his star rookie.

Atlanta quarterback Desmond Ridder pitched the ball to his right. Robinson grabbed it and burst toward the outside of the

Robinson stiff arms a Packers defender during Week 2 of the 2023 season.

offensive line. He sprinted ahead for 13 yards before going out of bounds. Atlanta scored a touchdown two plays later, right before halftime.

Robinson continued to create headaches for Green Bay in the second half. With the Falcons trailing by five in the fourth quarter, Ridder passed to Robinson near the right sideline. Corralling the ball, Robinson ran up the sideline for a 29-yard gain. The play helped set up a field goal that cut Atlanta's deficit to two.

The Falcons still trailed 24–22 with just over five minutes remaining. On a third-and-three play, Robinson lined up on the right like a wide receiver. He ran a sharp slant route toward the middle of the field, and Ridder found him for a 10-yard gain and a first down.

Atlanta kept marching down the field. However, the team soon faced fourth-and-one on Green Bay's 23 with 2:08 left. The safe play would have been to kick a field goal. That would give Atlanta the lead. Instead, Smith decided to go for a first down and try to draw more time off the clock before scoring. And he turned to his rookie running back to get the job done. Smith called the same pitch play that Atlanta ran on a fourth down earlier in the game. This time, the Packers were ready for it. Two defenders darted into the backfield, but Robinson juked left to make one miss. Then he rumbled ahead and avoided another tackler before going down after a 7-yard gain to keep the drive alive. Four plays later, with only 1:01 left, Atlanta kicker Younghoe Koo drilled the game-winning field goal.

NOT ENOUGH BIJAN

Bijan Robinson had a successful rookie season. But many Atlanta fans felt that coach Arthur Smith didn't use the star running back enough. In 2023, Robinson finished with 214 carries. The Falcons fired Smith after the season and hired Raheem Morris. With a new coach in charge, Robinson recorded 304 carries in 2024. He finished the season with 1,887 total yards.

Robinson finished the game against the Packers with 172 total yards. He went on to record 1,463 total yards during his rookie season. Robinson lived up to the high expectations placed on him, and the Falcons knew they had a superstar that they could build their offense around for years to come.

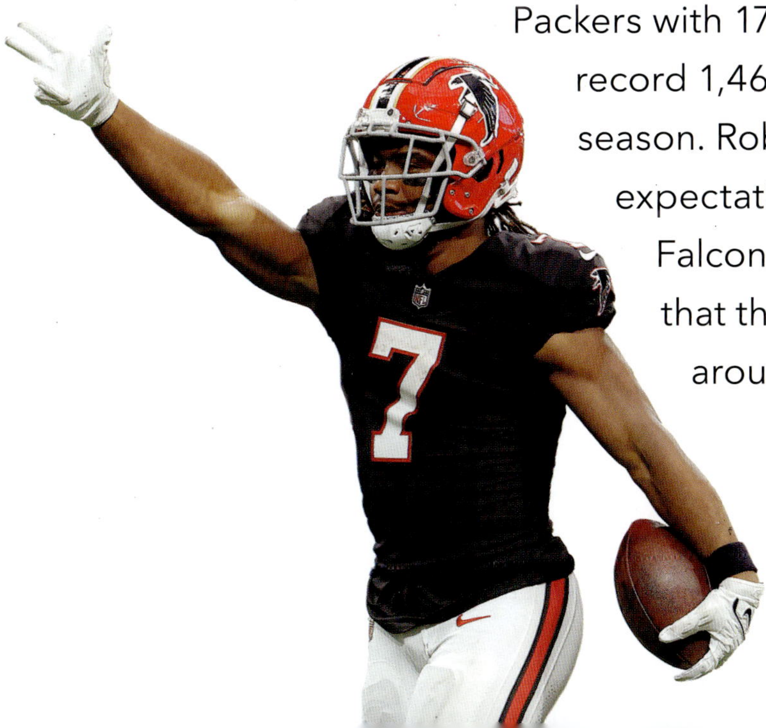

Robinson points after gaining a first down in the fourth quarter against the Packers.

NFL TEAMS MAP

NFC

NFC EAST

- DALLAS COWBOYS
- NEW YORK GIANTS
- PHILADELPHIA EAGLES
- WASHINGTON COMMANDERS

NFC WEST

- ARIZONA CARDINALS
- LOS ANGELES RAMS
- SAN FRANCISCO 49ERS
- SEATTLE SEAHAWKS

NFC NORTH

- CHICAGO BEARS
- DETROIT LIONS
- GREEN BAY PACKERS
- MINNESOTA VIKINGS

NFC SOUTH

- ATLANTA FALCONS
- CAROLINA PANTHERS
- NEW ORLEANS SAINTS
- TAMPA BAY BUCCANEERS

AFC

AFC EAST

- BUFFALO BILLS
- MIAMI DOLPHINS
- NEW ENGLAND PATRIOTS
- NEW YORK JETS

AFC WEST

- DENVER BRONCOS
- KANSAS CITY CHIEFS
- LAS VEGAS RAIDERS
- LOS ANGELES CHARGERS

AFC NORTH

- BALTIMORE RAVENS
- CINCINNATI BENGALS
- CLEVELAND BROWNS
- PITTSBURGH STEELERS

AFC SOUTH

- HOUSTON TEXANS
- INDIANAPOLIS COLTS
- JACKSONVILLE JAGUARS
- TENNESSEE TITANS

Atlanta Stadium hosted the Falcons for 26 years.

CHAPTER 2

HOT SPOT

ATLANTA HAD A LONG HISTORY HOSTING COLLEGE FOOTBALL AND MINOR league baseball. By the 1960s, the city emerged as a top candidate for professional football. Both the NFL and the upstart American Football League (AFL) saw Atlanta as a city on the rise. Atlanta mayor Ivan Allen wanted to prove that his city was ready to host a pro team. So, in 1963, he approved the construction of a new stadium.

Major League Baseball's Milwaukee Braves had agreed to move to Atlanta and play in the new stadium in 1966. And on June 7, the AFL awarded the city a team to begin playing during the 1966 season. Once NFL commissioner Pete Rozelle heard about that deal, he flew to Atlanta and offered Allen an NFL team that could start playing in 1966. Less than a month after receiving an AFL team, Allen agreed to

NFL commissioner Pete Rozelle, *left*, presents a certificate of NFL membership to Atlanta owner Rankin M. Smith in 1966.

Rozelle's deal. Atlanta would host an NFL team instead. On June 30, Atlanta businessman Rankin M. Smith bought the new NFL team for $8.5 million, equal to about $83.6 million in 2024.

Shortly after acquiring the team, Smith held a contest for fans to come up with a team name. Many fans suggested "Falcons," with one local teacher writing that the bird "is deadly and has a great sporting tradition." That convinced Smith to officially name the team the Atlanta Falcons.

SLOW START

Thousands of fans began buying season tickets to watch the Falcons. Meanwhile, the team started to build its roster. With the top pick in the 1966 draft, Atlanta selected two-way Texas star Tommy Nobis. He focused on playing linebacker in the NFL, and he

Linebacker Tommy Nobis starred for Atlanta from 1966 until 1976 and earned the nickname "Mr. Falcon."

quickly proved to be a tackling machine. Nobis racked up more than 20 tackles per game as a rookie and made the first of his five Pro Bowls.

While the Falcons had an instant star in Nobis, he didn't have a lot of talent around him. Most of Atlanta's players arrived through the expansion draft. Other NFL teams were able to protect their best players, allowing the Falcons to choose from the rest of their rosters. Falcons fans didn't mind, though. More than 54,000 of them packed Atlanta Stadium in Week 1 of the 1966 season to watch their team take on the Los Angeles Rams. Reality set in quickly, however, as the Rams jumped out to a 16–0 lead in the second quarter. While the Falcons battled back, they ended their first NFL game with a 19–14 loss.

Like most NFL expansion teams, the Falcons struggled to win games in their first season. While Nobis lived up to

Falcons quarterback Randy Johnson (11) scans the field against the Los Angeles Rams in 1967.

expectations on defense, the team's other first-round pick had a harder time. Quarterback Randy Johnson started seven of Atlanta's first 10 games. During those games, Johnson threw only seven touchdowns. With an 0–10 record, the Falcons traveled to New York to take on the Giants in Week 11. Atlanta's rookie quarterback was dialed in. Johnson's three touchdown passes helped the Falcons build a 20–3 lead. Then he ran for another score to secure a 27–16 win, Atlanta's first in the NFL.

TOUGHENING UP

During their first few seasons, the Falcons continued to pile up losses. However, the team made two key additions in 1968. The first was Claude Humphrey, who arrived with the third pick in the draft.

Defensive end Claude Humphrey, *right*, made six Pro Bowls with the Falcons.

The defensive lineman recorded 11 1/2 sacks in 1968 and earned NFL Defensive Rookie of the Year honors.

Despite having talented young stars in Nobis and Humphrey, Atlanta still had one of the worst defenses in the league. After starting the 1968 season 0–3, the Falcons made a key addition. Atlanta fired head coach Norb Hecker and replaced him with Norm Van Brocklin. A former star quarterback, Van Brocklin was a fiery coach. And while the Falcons won only two games in his first season, the new coach began to change Atlanta's fate.

During the 1971 season, the Falcons posted their first winning record, finishing 7–6–1. Following another seven-win season in 1972, Atlanta came into the 1973 season with some momentum. In Week 1, the Falcons faced their biggest rival, the Saints, in New Orleans. The game wasn't close. The Falcons pummeled the Saints, who committed eight turnovers, and cruised to a 62–7 win.

PLAYING FOR LEON

Atlanta running back Harmon Wages' father, Leon Wages, attended a 1969 Falcons game against the New Orleans Saints despite being in very poor health. Knowing this was likely the last time Leon would get to watch his son play, coach Norm Van Brocklin featured Harmon Wages heavily on offense. Wages threw for a 16-yard touchdown in the first quarter. Then in the second quarter, he caught an 88-yard touchdown pass. Wages capped off his day with a 66-yard score on the ground in the fourth quarter. He became the seventh player in NFL history to throw, catch, and rush for a touchdown in the same game.

Atlanta's momentum didn't last, however. The Falcons scored only 15 points in their next three games and fell to 1–3. But that led into a seven-game winning streak that included an upset over the undefeated Minnesota Vikings in Week 10. The Falcons seemed poised for their first playoff appearance. Once again, though, things fell apart.

Nobis (60) was named to five Pro Bowls with the Falcons from 1966 to 1976.

Atlanta ended their winning streak by losing two games, including a loss to the lowly St. Louis Cardinals. With a 9-5 record, the Falcons finished one win short of the playoffs.

LONG TIME COMING

Heading into the 1977 season, Atlanta still hadn't reached the playoffs, and few expected that to change. And Atlanta no longer had the stellar Nobis, who retired before the season. Meanwhile, promising quarterback Steve Bartkowski, who the Falcons had taken with the top pick in the 1975 draft, needed knee surgery that would keep him out for half of the season. On top of that, the Falcons were in their first season under the unproven head coach Leeman Bennett. At 39 years old, he was the youngest coach in the league at the time.

Leeman Bennett had served as an assistant coach for the Los Angeles Rams for four years before becoming head coach for the Falcons.

Bennett's lack of head-coaching experience didn't hinder his ability to game-plan. He decided the Falcons' defense should blitz as much as possible. The aggressive plan showed promise early. The Los Angeles Rams had dismantled the Falcons 59–0 late in the 1976 season. In the 1977 season opener, the Falcons held the Rams to 167 total yards in a 17–6 win. Atlanta's suffocating defense earned the nickname "Grits Blitz," combining the popular Southern dish with the team's defensive strategy. The Falcons set an NFL record by allowing only 9.2 points per game in 1977.

While the team's defense shut down opponents, Atlanta's offense continued to struggle. Even when Bartkowski returned as a starter in Week 8, the unit barely improved. Despite boasting a historic defense, the Falcons finished 7–7 and missed the playoffs again.

Falcons defensive back Rolland Lawrence recorded seven interceptions in 1977.

Still, Falcons fans had reasons to be optimistic. With largely the same roster as in 1976, Bennett had made the team much more competitive in 1977. That improvement continued in 1978. Bartkowski had lost the starting job but reclaimed it after Week 3, and Atlanta finished 9–7. Four of those wins came in the final 10 seconds of the game. Those close calls helped the Falcons clinch their first playoff berth in team history.

More than 49,000 fans showed up to watch the Falcons take on the Philadelphia Eagles at Atlanta–Fulton County Stadium. Under rainy skies, the Eagles built a 13–0 lead. That score remained with five minutes left in the fourth quarter. Then the Falcons' offense came alive.

Quarterback Steve Bartkowski threw for 2,489 yards in 1978.

Atlanta tight end Jim Mitchell tallied 366 receiving yards in 1978.

First, Bartkowski connected with tight end Jim Mitchell for a 20-yard touchdown. On Atlanta's next offensive drive, Bartkowski threw a 37-yard touchdown to receiver Wallace Francis to tie the game with 1:39 remaining. Falcons kicker Tim Mazzetti, who the Eagles had cut during training camp, made the extra point to put Atlanta ahead 14–13.

The Falcons just needed to stop the Eagles to secure their first playoff victory. Instead, the Eagles drove down the field and set up a 33-yard field-goal attempt. Punter Mike Michel lined up with a chance to win it for Philadelphia. But the kick sailed wide, sending Falcons fans into a frenzy. They rushed onto the field to celebrate their team's first ever playoff game victory.

The following week, the Falcons traveled to Dallas to take on the Cowboys. Almost no one expected the Falcons to beat the defending champion Cowboys. However, Bartkowski led two scoring drives late in the second quarter to give Atlanta a 20–13 lead at halftime. The experienced Cowboys responded in the second half, though, and won 27–20. The team's first playoff run had ended, but the future was finally looking bright in Atlanta.

Falcons fans run onto the field to celebrate winning their first playoff game.

Falcons running back William Andrews made four straight Pro Bowls starting in 1980.

CHAPTER 3

ON THE RISE

ATLANTA HAD BUILT ONE OF THE NFL'S STRONGEST DEFENSES UNDER coach Leeman Bennett. In the 1979 draft, the Falcons attempted to bolster their offense by selecting three running backs. One of them, third-round pick William Andrews, became Atlanta's leading rusher as a rookie. However, the Falcons followed their 1978 playoff run by going just 6–10.

By 1980, the team's playbook featured many options for receivers so they could change their routes based on what coverage the defense was running. With plenty of open receivers to throw to, Steve Bartkowski tossed a league-leading 31 touchdowns. It was a career high for Bartkowski. Meanwhile, the defense reloaded with rookie linebackers Buddy Curry and Al Richardson. That duo had a combined total of

Linebacker Buddy Curry (50) played eight seasons with the Falcons from 1980 to 1987.

10 interceptions and had become co-winners of the Defensive Rookie of the Year Award.

With a balanced roster, the Falcons won a team-record 12 games and clinched their first division title. That earned Atlanta a first-round bye in the playoffs, followed by a home game against the Dallas Cowboys. Atlanta's fans went into a frenzy when Bartkowski lofted a perfect pass to Alfred Jenkins for a 60-yard touchdown to take an early 10–0 lead. However, Dallas battled back to tie the game in the second quarter. The high-powered Falcons responded with two touchdown drives to take a 24–10 lead in the third quarter. After Dallas scored another touchdown, Tim Mazzetti kicked a field goal to put Atlanta up 27–17 in the fourth.

Once again, the Cowboys came back. Dallas receiver Drew Pearson scored to bring his team within three. Then, with

42 seconds left, Pearson caught another touchdown pass to give the Cowboys their first lead of the game. The once-rowdy crowd in Atlanta fell silent. The Cowboys left with a shocking 30–27 win.

Falcons running back William Andrews rushed for 1,308 yards in 1980.

Bartkowski and Andrews kept the Falcons' offense near the top of the league in the early 1980s. That duo led the Falcons back to the playoffs in 1982. But after the Falcons lost in the first round to the Minnesota Vikings, the team fired Bennett. Things only fell apart further after that.

Quarterback Steve Bartkowski walks off the field after the Falcons' loss in the 1980 playoffs.

In 1984, Andrews suffered a knee injury that would sideline him for two seasons and essentially end his career. In 1985, the Falcons benched Bartkowski and started the season 0–5. The Falcons eventually cut the quarterback, and Atlanta finished 4–12 for the second consecutive season.

PRIME TIME

The Falcons hosted the Los Angeles Rams to open the 1989 season. In the first quarter, Los Angeles punted to cornerback Deion Sanders. The Falcons' rookie dropped the ball. By the time he picked it up, a Rams defender had zeroed in on him. Sanders shook off the defender, then he avoided two more attempted tackles as he sprinted toward the right side of the field. With one swift cut back inside, Sanders found the lane he was searching for. He zoomed downfield for a 68-yard touchdown to put the Falcons ahead 7–0.

Cornerback Deion Sanders recorded 24 interceptions with the Falcons from 1989 to 1993.

It was an electrifying start for one of the league's most thrilling players. The Falcons had picked Sanders fifth in the 1989 draft. Nicknamed "Prime Time," Sanders used his speed and agility to become a shutdown cornerback and one of the game's all-time great kick returners.

Though Sanders was an immediate star, the Falcons stumbled to a 3–13 record in 1989. They held the top pick in the 1990 draft. However, the Falcons traded it to the Indianapolis Colts for a future pick and multiple players, including Andre Rison. The wide receiver was coming off a successful rookie season with the Colts, and he fit right

Falcons wide receiver Andre Rison reached the Pro Bowl every year from 1990 to 1993.

in with the Falcons. He racked up 1,208 receiving yards to make the Pro Bowl while helping improve Atlanta's offense.

Jerry Glanville coached the Houston Oilers for five years before becoming Atlanta's head coach.

TEAM IN BLACK

While Sanders and Rison set the standard for the Falcons on the field, new coach Jerry Glanville made his presence known on the sideline. Glanville had served as the team's defensive backs coach during the Grits Blitz era in the late 1970s. Typically dressed in all black, he brought an edgy attitude to the Falcons. While he demanded hard work from his players, he also wanted the game to be fun. That turned out to be the perfect fit on a team that featured big personalities in Sanders and Rison.

The Falcons made another big change in 1990, trading their red home jerseys for black ones. "We wore black uniforms because black wasn't a color, it was an attitude," Glanville later said. The Falcons showcased that attitude. After eight straight losing seasons, the Falcons finished 10–6 in 1991 and clinched a spot in the playoffs.

"WE WORE BLACK UNIFORMS BECAUSE BLACK WASN'T A COLOR, IT WAS AN ATTITUDE."

—JERRY GLANVILLE

In the first round, the Falcons traveled to New Orleans to take on the Saints. Atlanta had already won once at the Superdome

Sanders dons a black home jersey during a game in 1991.

that season, defeating the Saints in overtime. The return trip was just as difficult. New Orleans jumped out to an early 7-0 lead in the first quarter. The Saints then drove into the red zone on their next possession looking to go up two scores. Instead, Sanders intercepted a pass in the end zone. By halftime, Rison had scored a touchdown and the Falcons trailed 13-10.

Another Atlanta receiver soon stole the spotlight. Despite growing up in New Orleans, Michael Haynes had rooted against the Saints his entire life. So when the Falcons drafted him in 1988, he said he was thrilled to play against the Saints twice each season.

Falcons wide receiver Michael Haynes recorded a career-high 1,122 receiving yards in 1991.

Haynes hauled in a 20-yard touchdown in the third quarter to give the Falcons a 17-13 lead. Later, with the game tied 20-20 and under three minutes left, quarterback Chris Miller passed to Haynes near midfield. The receiver cut to his left to avoid a tackle, then burst down the field for a 61-yard game-winning touchdown. "Going home as a native and playing against the team you grew up watching . . . I loved going in there and beating those guys," Haynes said.

A long playoff run would have to wait, however. The following week, Washington thumped the Falcons 24–7. Everything began to unravel after that. After finishing 6–10 in the 1992 and 1993 seasons, the team fired Glanville. Sanders was fed up with losing and left Atlanta in free agency. Rison stuck around for the 1994 season, the final year of his contract. When the Falcons couldn't offer him a large enough extension, he signed with the Cleveland Browns before the 1995 season. Suddenly, the team that had invigorated Atlanta had fallen apart.

TWO-SPORT STAR

Five days before making his NFL debut, Deion Sanders hit a home run while playing for the New York Yankees. Throughout most seasons of his NFL career, Sanders also played for a Major League Baseball (MLB) team. On October 11, 1992, he even tried to play in both leagues on the same day. That afternoon, Sanders played for the Falcons in Miami in a 21–17 loss to the Dolphins. He then flew to Pittsburgh and suited up for the Atlanta Braves as they took on the Pirates in a playoff game. Having arrived 16 minutes before first pitch, Sanders didn't play in a 7–1 loss.

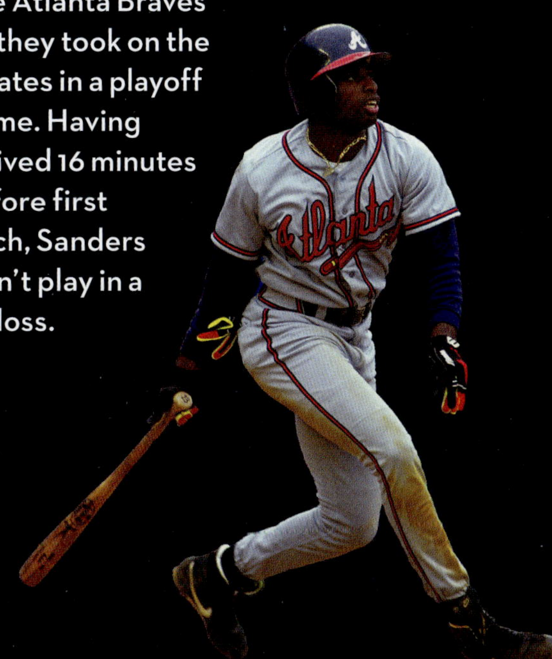

Falcons quarterback Chris Chandler threw for 2,692 yards in 1997.

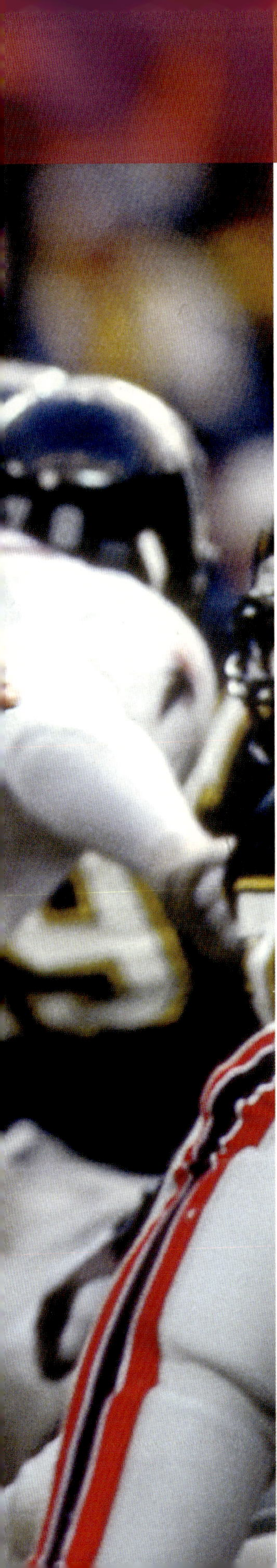

CHAPTER 4

DIRTY BIRDS

Over their first 31 seasons, the Falcons never advanced past the second round of the playoffs. Prior to the 1997 season, the team brought in Dan Reeves to change that. Reeves had won 141 games in 16 years as a head coach. The Falcons hired him as head coach and general manager, hoping his experience could help get them back to the playoffs.

One reason for Atlanta's struggles was instability at the quarterback position. Reeves set out to fix this problem. He sent two draft picks to the Houston Oilers for veteran Chris Chandler. Still, the Reeves era got off to a slow start when the team lost its first five games in 1997. But after finishing the season with seven wins in their final 11 games, the Falcons went into the 1998 season with optimism.

When the season began, the Falcons looked like a different team. Fifth-year running back Jamal Anderson took a starring role. The former seventh-round draft pick bulldozed his way to 1,846 yards on a league-high 410 carries. When defenses tried to stop Anderson, Chandler was able to pick them apart with deep throws downfield.

Running back Jamal Anderson scored 16 total touchdowns in 1998.

Despite Atlanta's 6–2 record, halfway through the season, few considered the Falcons a serious contender. Most of the team's wins had come against weaker opponents. The Falcons set out to prove themselves in a Week 10 matchup against the New England Patriots.

Atlanta tight end O. J. Santiago scored two touchdowns in the 41–10 domination of New England. After one of them, he flapped his arms in the end zone and chirped like a bird. Following the game, Santiago went into the locker room and asked, "How about

Tight end O. J. Santiago does "the Dirty Bird" dance after scoring a touchdown in 1998.

them Dirty Birds?" For the rest of the season, Atlanta players started doing "the Dirty Bird" dance after scoring touchdowns.

DEEP RUN

The carefree Falcons ripped off a nine-game win streak to finish the regular season 14–2. But in their first playoff game, the Falcons

Anderson dives into the end zone against the 49ers in a playoff game on January 9, 1999.

hosted the San Francisco 49ers. It was a tough matchup. The 49ers had regularly beaten up on the Falcons during the 1990s.

Anderson erased any concerns the 70,262 fans in the Georgia Dome had. His two rushing touchdowns put the Falcons up 14–0 in the first half. Though the experienced 49ers battled back, the Falcons held on to win 20–18. For the first time, Atlanta was headed to the National Football Conference (NFC) Championship Game.

In most seasons, Atlanta's record would have been good enough for the top seed. But in 1998, the Minnesota Vikings won 15 games while boasting the highest scoring offense in NFL history. The Falcons entered the NFC title game in Minneapolis on a 10-game win streak. Yet almost everyone expected the Vikings to overpower Atlanta and cruise to the Super Bowl.

Anderson rushes during the NFC title game against Minnesota on January 17, 1999.

Once again, the Falcons weren't fazed. After the Falcons received the opening kickoff, Chandler led Atlanta on a 12-play drive that he capped off with a touchdown pass to Anderson. Minnesota fans loudly booed as Anderson performed the Dirty Bird in the end zone. The Vikings responded, though, scoring a touchdown on their first drive. And while Atlanta's offense stalled, the Vikings scored on their next three drives to take a 20–7 lead.

Atlanta's defense kept the Falcons in the game. The Falcons forced a fumble near the end of the first half. Chandler converted it into a touchdown pass to head into halftime trailing 20–14.

The Falcons continued to hang with the Vikings in the second half. Kicker Morten Andersen nailed a pair of field goals, with the second bringing Atlanta to within seven points. However, things looked bleak with a little over two minutes left when Gary Anderson trotted onto the field. Minnesota's kicker was in the midst of a historic season. He hadn't missed a field goal in his last 122 kicks. If he delivered again from 38 yards, the Vikings would go up by 10 points and all but seal the victory. Instead, Anderson pulled the ball wide left, keeping Atlanta alive.

Chandler looks to make a pass during the NFC Championship Game.

With new life, Chandler and the Falcons drove 71 yards. Atlanta tied the game 27–27 when the quarterback connected with Terance Mathis for a 16-yard score with 49 seconds left. The Vikings tried to answer but ultimately took a knee, sending the game into overtime.

Atlanta's dramatic comeback seemed to be all for naught when the Vikings won the coin toss to start overtime. All Minnesota's explosive offense needed was a field goal to send them to the Super Bowl. However, the Falcons' defense forced the Vikings to punt twice in overtime. The second stop set up Atlanta's offense on its own 9-yard line. Behind Jamal Anderson's powerful running and a pair of big catches from Santiago, the Falcons drove down the field. They got to the Vikings' 21-yard line, and Andersen came on to try a 39-yard field goal. He drilled it, sending the Falcons to their first Super Bowl.

Wide receiver Terance Mathis (81) celebrates scoring in the NFC Championship Game.

Kicker Morten Andersen celebrates sending the Falcons to Super Bowl XXXIII.

But Atlanta would have to battle if they wanted the Lombardi Trophy. The defending champion Denver Broncos awaited in Super Bowl XXXIII. In legendary quarterback John Elway's final season, his Broncos arrived as heavy favorites. The Falcons once again scored on their opening drive, with Andersen kicking a field goal. But Denver was relentless after that. The Broncos cruised to their second straight title with a 34–19 victory, ending Atlanta's dream run.

Chandler is sacked as he throws during Super Bowl XXXIII on January 31, 1999.

VICK MANIA

After winning 14 games in the 1998 season, Atlanta won only 16 games over the next three seasons combined. In search of a spark, the Falcons traded up to get the top pick in the 2001 draft. With it, they selected game-changing quarterback Michael Vick. His combination of a strong arm and elite scrambling had made him a sensation at Virginia Tech. The Falcons hoped his skills would translate into the NFL.

After starting two games as a rookie, Vick won the starting job ahead of the 2002 season. While dual-threat quarterbacks had played in the NFL for decades, the league had never witnessed anyone like Vick. He rushed for 777 yards in 2002. He ran for 173 yards in a win over Minnesota, including a 46-yard run in overtime. That broke a 51-year-old record for most rushing yards in a game by a quarterback. "Michael was a rock star playing football," Falcons general manager Rich McKay said. All of his highlights helped the Falcons pick up wins too. Atlanta went 9–6–1 and returned to the playoffs for the first time since 1998.

"MICHAEL WAS A ROCK STAR PLAYING FOOTBALL."

—RICH MCKAY

The Falcons traveled to historic Lambeau Field to take on the Green Bay Packers. Not only were the Packers undefeated at home in 2002, but they had never lost a playoff game at Lambeau. The weather provided an even bigger advantage for Green Bay, as the teams played in below-freezing temperatures. But when the game started, something unexpected happened. The Falcons appeared comfortable in the cold. Vick racked up

In 2002, quarterback Michael Vick threw for 2,936 yards.

181 total yards and a touchdown, while Atlanta's defense forced five turnovers. The Falcons' 27–7 upset win stunned the league. However, the Philadelphia Eagles ended the Falcons' season the following week with a 20–6 rout.

Falcons running back Warrick Dunn ran for 142 yards against the Rams in the playoffs after the 2004 season.

A NEW LEADER

After an injury shortened his 2003 season, Vick returned to showcase his amazing skills in 2004. He led the Falcons to 11 wins and their first division title since 1998. The St. Louis Rams came to town for the playoffs. Vick accounted for 119 of the team's 327 rushing yards in a blowout 47–17 win. But once again, the Eagles contained Vick the next week, leaving the Falcons one win short of reaching the Super Bowl.

Vick had established himself as one of the NFL's top quarterbacks. After earning a third Pro Bowl selection in 2005, he became the first quarterback to rush for more than 1,000 yards in a season in 2006. Atlanta fans adored their franchise quarterback, and Vick's exciting play made him one of the biggest stars in the NFL. Then his stardom came crashing down.

SHORT STAY

In January 2007, the Falcons hired Bobby Petrino as head coach. The team hoped that the former University of Louisville coach could get the best out of Michael Vick. Instead, three different quarterbacks started for the Falcons in Vick's absence that season. A loss to the New Orleans Saints left the Falcons 3-10. Two days later, Petrino resigned to become the head coach at the University of Arkansas. Instead of addressing the team face-to-face about his decision, Petrino left a note in each player's locker.

In April 2007, police arrested Vick on charges related to a dogfighting operation run out of his house. A judge sentenced him to 23 months in prison. The NFL suspended him indefinitely.

Without their star quarterback, the Falcons won only four games in 2007. They were in desperate need of a new quarterback. The Falcons hoped they'd found one when they used their third pick to select former Boston College star Matt Ryan in the 2008 draft.

Quarterback Matt Ryan threw 16 touchdowns in 2008.

Falcons quarterback Matt Ryan won the Offensive Rookie of the Year Award in 2008.

CHAPTER 5

FLYING HIGH

THE FALCONS CAME INTO THE 2008 SEASON WITH A NEW HEAD COACH, Mike Smith. And he began his first season by making rookie Matt Ryan his starting quarterback. The decision paid off immediately. Ryan completed his first pass in the NFL for a 62-yard touchdown. Running down the field in celebration, Ryan waved his arms up and down to pump up the home crowd.

Atlanta had surrounded Ryan with talented athletes. Fourth-year wide receiver Roddy White seemed to catch every pass that came his way, and he quickly became Ryan's favorite target. Meanwhile, speedy running back Michael Turner signed with Atlanta that season and immediately became an important part of the offense.

Relying on his accurate arm and awareness in the pocket, Ryan helped the Falcons go 11–5 and reach the playoffs in 2008. The rookie's inexperience showed up there, as he threw two interceptions in a loss to the Arizona Cardinals. But the Falcons knew they had hit the jackpot with Ryan, and they continued to build up the offense. Before the 2009 season, Atlanta traded for future Hall of Fame tight end Tony Gonzalez.

Tight end Tony Gonzalez made four Pro Bowls with the Falcons from 2010 to 2013.

After missing the playoffs in 2009, Atlanta raced to an NFC-best 13 wins in 2010. However, a shocking 48–21 loss to the Green Bay Packers in the playoffs ended the Falcons' season. Though the loss was disappointing, Falcons management believed the team was close to winning a championship. To help take that next step, the Falcons traded up in the 2011 draft and selected Julio Jones.

The amazingly athletic wide receiver had been a hero at Alabama. And he fit in seamlessly with Atlanta's stacked offense. White and Jones quickly formed one of the league's most feared wide receiver duos. They helped Atlanta win 10 games in 2011, giving the team back-to-back playoff berths for the first time. Then the Falcons came back with 13 wins and a division title in 2012.

Falcons wide receiver Julio Jones, *right*, caught 79 passes for 1,198 yards and 10 touchdowns in 2012.

In the divisional round, the Falcons hosted the Seattle Seahawks, who had given up the fewest points that season. Seattle's defense failed to slow Atlanta. Late in the second quarter, Ryan launched a deep pass to White for a 47-yard touchdown to put Atlanta up 20–0.

By the start of the fourth quarter, the Falcons led 27–7. A trip to the NFC Championship Game seemed guaranteed. But the Seahawks responded with two touchdown drives. With the Falcons' offense unable to get a drive going, Seattle scored another touchdown with 31 seconds left to take a 28–27 lead.

Since his days playing high school football, Ryan's teammates had called him "Matty Ice" for keeping his cool under pressure. That nickname was tested as he took the field trailing by one. On his first dropback, Ryan lofted a pass to wide receiver Harry Douglas for a 22-yard gain. Then Ryan fired a pass over the middle to Gonzalez for another 19 yards. That allowed kicker Matt Bryant to nail a 49-yard field goal and secure Atlanta's first playoff win in eight years.

Kicker Matt Bryant celebrates his game-winning field goal against the Seahawks on January 13, 2013.

The Falcons hosted the San Francisco

49ers in the NFC Championship Game a week later. Early in the second quarter, Jones caught his second touchdown pass of the game to put the Falcons up 17-0. The chance to go to the Super Bowl slipped away from the Falcons, though, as the 49ers came back to stun Atlanta 28-24.

OFFENSIVE GENIUS

The Falcons had posted a winning record in each of Smith's first five seasons. However, following the crushing playoff loss, the Falcons collapsed. After consecutive losing seasons in 2013 and 2014, the Falcons fired Smith and replaced him with Dan Quinn.

Quinn, who had served as Seattle's defensive coordinator, set about fixing Atlanta's defense. Offensive coordinator Kyle Shanahan took the lead on the other side. Regarded as one of the league's best signal-callers, Shanahan wasted no time utilizing Jones's size and speed. In 2015, Jones led the NFL with 136 catches and 1,871 yards.

After a bounce-back 8-8 season in 2015, the Falcons boasted the league's

EMOTIONAL WIN

Few tight ends in history could match Tony Gonzalez's production. But one thing kept eluding him: playoff success. In 12 years with the Kansas City Chiefs, Gonzalez lost all three playoff games he played in. Then, after he was traded to Atlanta, the Falcons lost their first playoff games after the 2010 and 2011 seasons. Finally, the Falcons beat the Seattle Seahawks in the playoffs after the 2012 season. Gonzalez couldn't hold back tears after finally experiencing a playoff win 16 years into his career.

highest-scoring offense in 2016. Ryan, who racked up career-best numbers, earned NFL Most Valuable Player (MVP) honors and lifted the Falcons to 11 wins and a division title. Then, in two home playoff games, Ryan threw for 730 yards and seven touchdowns as the Falcons blew out the Seahawks and the Packers. Just like that, the Falcons were back in the Super Bowl.

Ryan threw for 4,944 yards and 38 touchdowns in 2016.

WRONG SIDE OF HISTORY

Super Bowl LI featured Atlanta's offense against the New England Patriots' defense. The Falcons scored the most points in the league while New England allowed the fewest. After a slow start, Ryan found his groove on Atlanta's third drive. The MVP connected with Jones for two long gains. Then running back Devonta Freeman gashed New England on three straight runs and scored the game's opening touchdown. After a quick three-and-out by the Patriots, Ryan completed three more long passes, including a 19-yard touchdown to tight end Austin Hooper. In the middle of the third quarter, Ryan threw another touchdown pass, this time to running back Tevin Coleman to put the Falcons up 28–3.

Running back Devonta Freeman dives into the end zone during Super Bowl LI on February 5, 2017.

After years of struggles, Atlanta appeared to be cruising to its first championship. There was just one problem: New England quarterback Tom Brady was one of the best in NFL history. He'd already led the Patriots to four Super Bowl titles, and he wasn't about to give up on a fifth. Facing an Atlanta defense that ranked near the bottom of the league in points allowed, Brady finally found his footing.

Cornerback Robert Alford (23) returns an interception 82 yards for a touchdown during Super Bowl LI.

Brady led two straight scoring drives to cut the deficit to 28–12. When the Falcons got the ball back, the Patriots sacked Ryan, forced a fumble, and recovered it. With a short field to work with, Brady soon threw another touchdown. Suddenly, the Patriots trailed by only eight with 5:56 left in the game.

The Falcons offense retook the field knowing just one more score would likely seal the win. Ryan started the drive with a play-action pass to Freeman, who scurried down the field for 39 yards. Two plays later, Ryan escaped the pocket and fired a pass toward Jones near the right sideline. The 6-foot-3-inch receiver leaped high into the air to snag the ball. Then he gracefully tapped both feet inbounds for a 27-yard gain.

Jones hauls in a catch in the fourth quarter during Super Bowl LI.

The spectacular catch put the Falcons well into field-goal range. But on its next three plays, Atlanta lost 23 yards. Instead of scoring three points to go up by 11, the Falcons punted back to the Patriots with 3:38 remaining.

Brady made Atlanta pay. He led a 10-play touchdown drive capped off with a game-tying two-point conversion. The Falcons got the ball back with 52 seconds left, but they couldn't take the lead. For the first time in Super Bowl history, the game headed to overtime.

The offense that had carried Atlanta's season had stalled in the most crucial moments on football's biggest stage. And in overtime, that offense didn't even have an opportunity. Brady marched the Patriots down the field, and running back James White dove into the end zone to complete the biggest comeback in Super Bowl history. "There's nothing you can really say. That's a tough loss," Ryan said. "It's hard to find words tonight."

"THERE'S NOTHING YOU CAN REALLY SAY. THAT'S A TOUGH LOSS."

—MATT RYAN

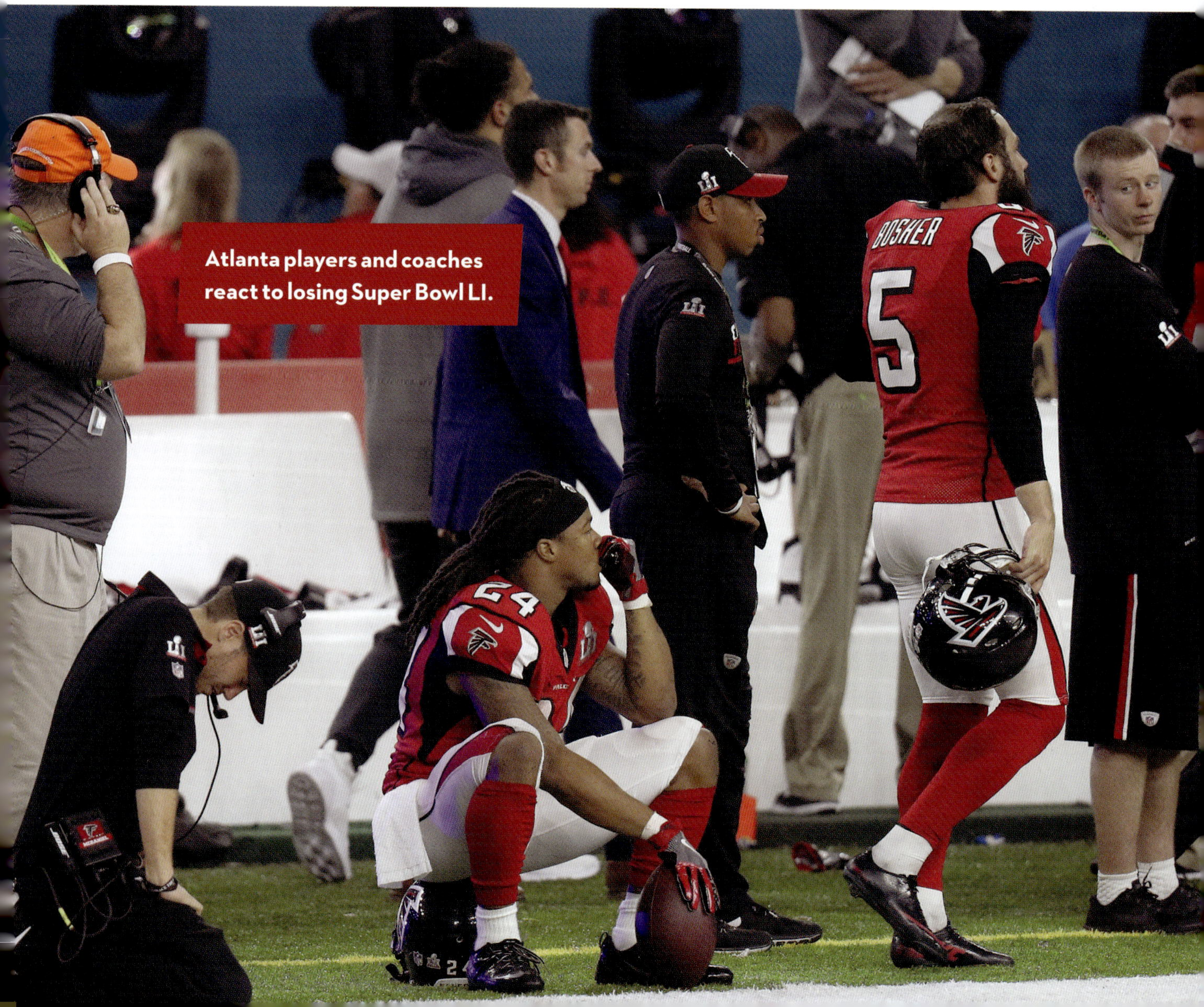

Atlanta players and coaches react to losing Super Bowl LI.

RELOADING ON OFFENSE

The Falcons bounced back from the devastating Super Bowl loss with a run to the playoffs in 2017, but they lost in the first round. Despite solid play from Ryan for the next few years, he never led the Falcons back to the playoffs. Following a 7–10 record in 2021, Atlanta traded the quarterback to the Indianapolis Colts. It was time to rebuild.

The Falcons began stockpiling talent in the draft. Over the next three seasons, Atlanta added versatile tight end Kyle Pitts, physical wide receiver Drake London, and shifty running back Bijan Robinson with top-10 picks. The team's leadership believed

Falcons running back Bijan Robinson recorded 1,463 total yards as a rookie in 2023.

FALCONS TROPHY CASE

SUPER BOWL CHAMPIONSHIPS: 0

CONFERENCE CHAMPIONSHIPS: 2

1998, 2016

DIVISION TITLES: 6

NFC West: 1980, 1998
NFC South: 2004, 2010, 2012, 2016

All stats are through the 2024 season.

the Falcons were ready to contend again in 2024. To lead the way, they signed veteran quarterback Kirk Cousins. However, the team surprised many by also using the eighth pick in that year's draft on a quarterback, Michael Penix.

That proved to be the start of a chaotic season. Though Cousins shined early, the losses and interceptions began to pile up. So, with three weeks to go, the Falcons made another shocking move.

Once seen as the quarterback of the future, Penix was thrust into the starting role. Though unable to get the Falcons into the playoffs, Penix showed flashes of promise. Falcons fans hoped he could be the one to finally bring a Super Bowl title to Atlanta.

Falcons quarterback Michael Penix threw three touchdowns in 2024.

TIMELINE

1966
The Atlanta Falcons play their first NFL season.

1978
In their 13th season, the Falcons reach the playoffs for the first time.

1981
After winning their first division title, the Falcons blow a fourth-quarter lead and lose to the Dallas Cowboys in the playoffs on January 4.

1991
The Falcons beat the Saints on December 28 in New Orleans for their first playoff win in 13 years.

1999
Atlanta defeats the Minnesota Vikings 30–27 in overtime on January 17 to reach the Super Bowl but falls to the Denver Broncos.

2003
Quarterback Michael Vick helps the Falcons become the first road team to ever win a playoff game at Lambeau Field on January 4.

2006
Vick becomes the first quarterback in NFL history to run for 1,000 yards in a season.

Atlanta drafts quarterback Matt Ryan, who leads the team to the playoffs as a rookie.
2008

2011
The Falcons trade up in the draft to select wide receiver Julio Jones with the sixth pick.

2013
Ryan leads a game-winning drive against the Seattle Seahawks on January 13 to earn his first win in the playoffs.

The Falcons blow a 28-3 lead against the New England Patriots in Super Bowl LI on February 5.
2017

Rookie quarterback Michael Penix takes over as the Falcons' starter for the final three games of the season.
2024

GLOSSARY

contract–an agreement to play for a certain team.

coordinator–an assistant coach who is in charge of the offense, defense, or special teams.

debut–first appearance.

draft–a system that allows teams to acquire new players coming into the league.

era–a period of time in history.

expansion draft–a special draft held to stock a new team using players from existing teams in the same league.

franchise quarterback–a quarterback capable of leading a team for a number of years.

general manager–an executive who runs a team and is responsible for finding and signing players.

momentum–the strength or force that allows something to continue or to grow stronger.

overtime–an extra period of play when the score is tied after regulation.

play-action pass–a play in which the quarterback fakes a handoff before dropping back to pass.

red zone–the area of the field between the 20-yard line and the goal line.

resign–to leave a job.

retire–to end one's career.

rival—an opponent with whom a player or team has a fierce and ongoing competition.

rookie—a professional athlete in his or her first year of competition.

roster—a list of players who make up a team.

upset—an unexpected victory by a supposedly weaker team or player.

veteran—someone who has played for many years.

ONLINE RESOURCES

Booklinks
NONFICTION NETWORK
FREE! ONLINE NONFICTION RESOURCES

To learn more about the Atlanta Falcons, please visit **abdobooklinks.com** or scan this QR code. These links are routinely monitored and updated to provide the most current information available.

INDEX